Spaceships and Rockets

By Deborah Lock

Series Editor Deborah Lock
US Senior Editor Shannon Beatty
Art Director Martin Wilson
Picture Researcher Surya Sarangi
Producer, Pre-production Nadine King

Reading Consultant Linda Gambrell, Ph.D.

First American Edition, 2016
Published in the United States by DK Publishing
345 Hudson Street, New York, New York 10014

Copyright © 2016 Dorling Kindersley Limited
DK, a Division of Penguin Random House LLC
16 17 18 19 10 9 8 7 6 5 4 3 2 1
001—280410–June/2016

A catalog record for this book is available from the Library of Congress.
ISBN: 978-1-4654-4511-7 (Paperback)
ISBN: 978-1-4654-4512-4 (Hardcover)

Printed and bound in China
DK books are available at special discounts when purchased in bulk for sales promotions,
premiums, fund-raising, or educational use. For details, contact: DK Publishing Special Markets,
345 Hudson Street, New York, New York 10014 or SpecialSales@dk.com.

The publisher would like to thank the following for their kind permission to reproduce their photographs:
(Key: a-above; b-below/bottom; c-center; f-far; l-left; r-right; t-top)
1 ESA: CNES / ARIANESPACE–Optique Photo Video du CSG, P. Baudon, 2013. 4-5 ESA: ESA–S. Corvaja,
2014. 6 Corbis: 2 / InterNetwork Media / Ocean (tc). 6-7 ESA: CNES / ARIANESPACE-Optique Photo Video du
CSG, 2013 (b). 8 ESA: ESA–S. Corvaja, 2013. 9 Science Photo Library: David Ducros. 10-11 Science Photo
Library: David Ducros / ESA. 12 ESA: ESA–D. Ducros, 2014. 13 Corbis: NASA. 14-15 ESA: ESA–S. Corvaja,
2014 (Background). 16-17 Science Photo Library: Ria Novosti. 16 Corbis: 2 / InterNetwork Media / Ocean (t).
17 Rex Features: Sovfoto / Universal Images Group (c). 18-19 NASA. 19 Science Photo Library: Friedrich
Saurer (cb). 20-21 NASA. 21 NASA: (t). 22-23 NASA: Carla Cioffi. 23 Getty Images: ATLAN Jean-Louis /
Contributor (c). 24 Corbis: NASA / CNP (tl). NASA: (b). 24-25 ESA: ESA–S. Corvaja, 2014 (Background).
NASA: (t). 25 NASA: (tr, b). 26 Corbis: 2 / InterNetwork Media / Ocean (t). NASA: (b). 26-27 ESA: ESA–J.
Huart, 2014 (b). 27 ESA: ESA–J. Huart, 2014 (cl, cr). 28-29 ESA: C.Carreau. 30 Science Photo Library: Julian
Baum. 31 NASA: JPL. 32 NASA: KSC. 32-33 Corbis: Elena Duvernay / Stocktrek Images. 34-35 ESA: ESA–S.
Corvaja, 2014. 36 Corbis: 2 / InterNetwork Media / Ocean (t). Getty Images: Frederic J. Brown / Staff (b). 37
Marsscientific.com: Clay Center Observatory (t). 38 Science Photo Library: Detlev Van Ravenswaay (cl). 38-39
Reaction Engines Limited / Adrian Mann. 39 Science Photo Library: Detlev Van Ravenswaay (ca). 40
Inspiration Mars: (t). 40-41 Science Photo Library: Walter Myers. 42-43 ESA: ESA–S. Corvaja, 2014. 42 Rex
Features: Courtesy Everett Collection (cb); SNAP (cla, cra). Endpapers: Dorling Kindersley: Robin
Hunter. Jacket images: Front: Corbis: Victor Habbick Visions / Science Photo Library br;
Getty Images: Stocktrek; NASA: tr; Back: ESA: J.Huart tr; Science Photo Library:
FRIEDRICH SAURER bl, SPUTNIK tl
All other images © Dorling Kindersley Limited
For further information see: www.dkimages.com

A WORLD OF IDEAS:
SEE ALL THERE IS TO KNOW
www.dk.com.

Contents

Parts of a Rocket

Rockets are made up of many parts, or stages. The **booster** rockets give extra power for launch.

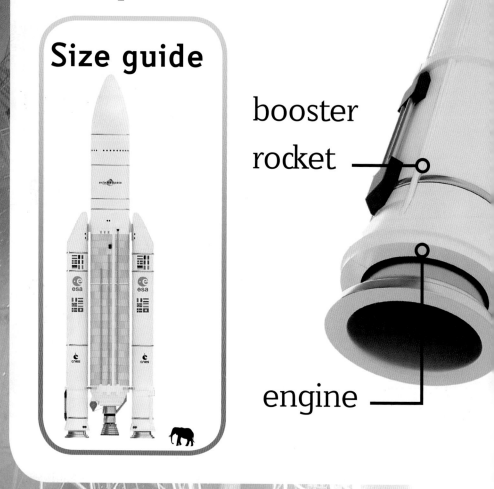

Size guide

booster rocket ——○

engine ——

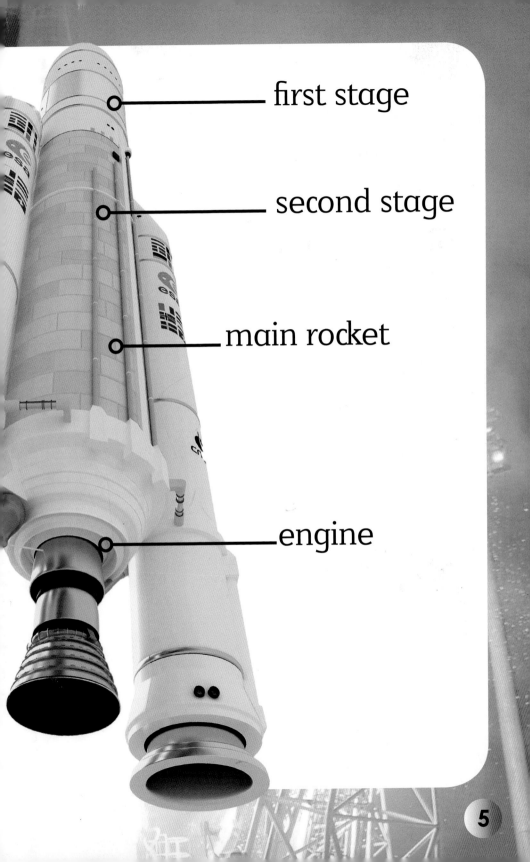

first stage

second stage

main rocket

engine

Chapter 1
The Launch

5

The rocket points to the sky. It is ready to launch.

4

The engines spark.
Flames and smoke
billow out.

3

The rocket shakes
and rumbles.

2

The engines roar.

1

Blastoff!

Up, up! The rocket
zooms into the sky.

The engines power the
rocket higher and higher.
The rocket looks like a tiny
speck in the sky. The boosters
drop away.

The rocket fires its smaller engine. It zooms upward, faster and faster.

It passes through the thin
layer of gases around Earth.
The rocket breaks through
into the darkness of space.

Each rocket that blasts off
has a job to do—a mission.

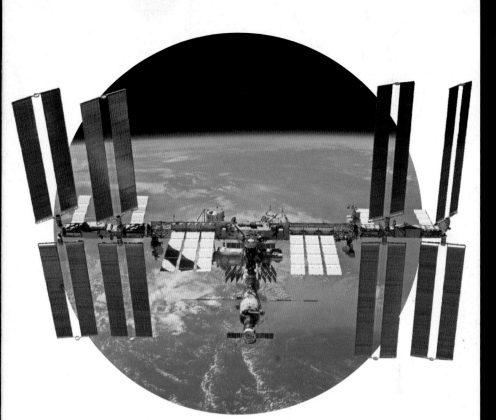

These missions can last a few days or a few weeks. Some missions can last for years and years.

Launch Sites

Countries around the world launch rockets. Here are some of the launch sites.

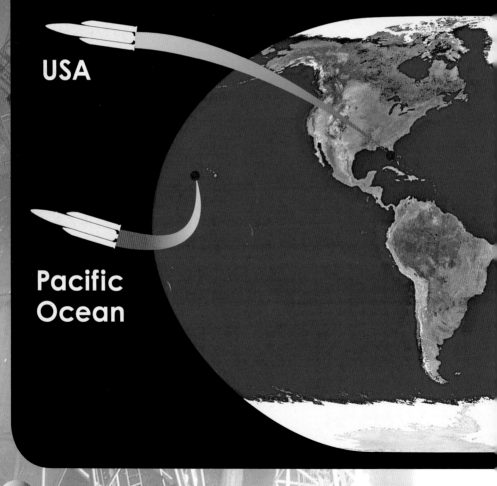

USA

Pacific Ocean

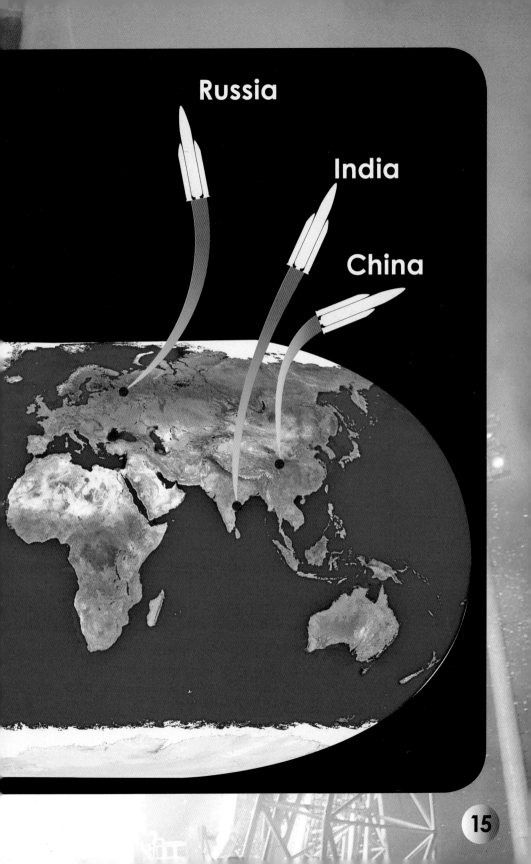

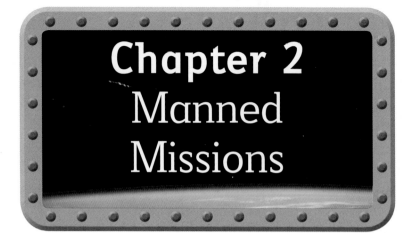

Chapter 2
Manned
Missions

Some rockets carry
people into space.
This rocket is called
Vostok 1 [VOH-stock].

It took the first person into space in 1961. His name was Yuri Gagarin [YOUR-ee ga-GAR-een]. He was Russian.

The *Saturn V* (5) rocket took people to the Moon. It was the largest rocket ever built. The **astronauts** sat in a small **capsule** called *Apollo 11*. This capsule was on the top of the rocket.

This is the space shuttle.
It took off on a rocket and
landed as a plane. It was
used to take astronauts
into space many times.

These astronauts visited the **space station** and did space walks.

Some rockets now take
tourists for a trip into space.
This is the Russian rocket
Soyuz [SU-yoos].

At the top is a **spacecraft** that takes people to the International Space Station. They stay for a week.

Visit the International Space Station

1-week trip
Price:
$50 million

work in the **lab**

 eat space food

keep fit

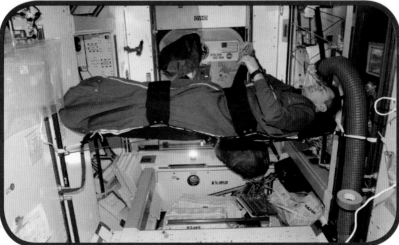

strap in to sleep

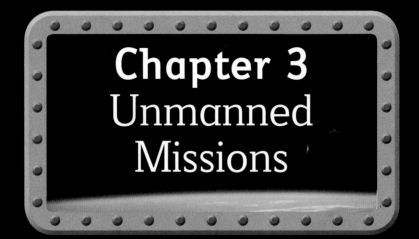

Chapter 3
Unmanned Missions

Some rockets carry satellites and probes into space. Satellites are machines. They travel around, or **orbit**, Earth.

Satellites send back pictures and messages to Earth. The *Ariane 5* [ah-ree-AH-ne] rocket can carry two heavy satellites.

Probes are small, unmanned spacecraft. These probes fly to planets and explore space. They send back pictures and other data to Earth. The *Rosetta* [roh-SET-tah] probe flew past asteroids.

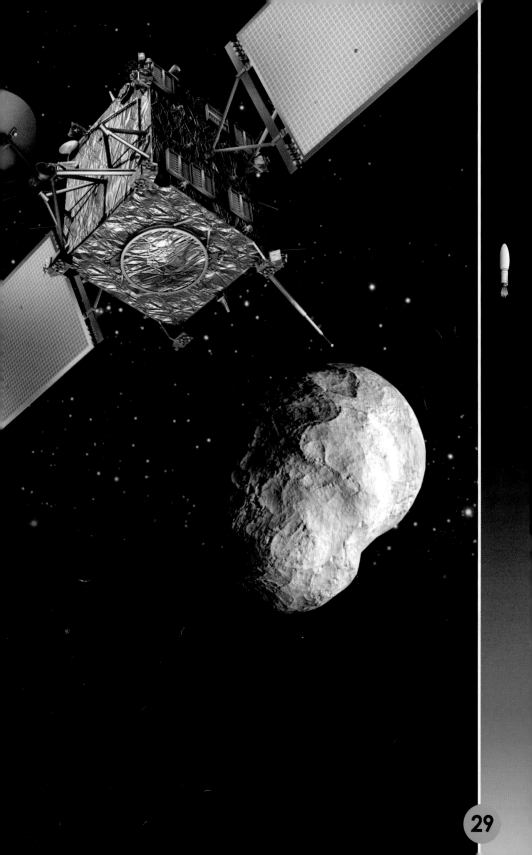

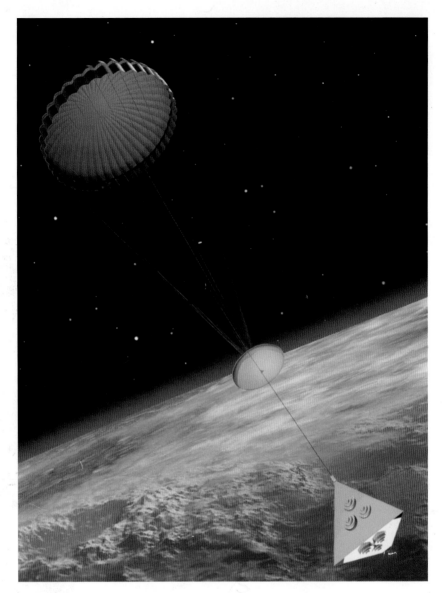

The *Pathfinder* probe
landed on Mars in 1997.
It needed a very large
parachute to slow down.

It landed a small robotic vehicle called a **rover**. This was the first robot to do tests on the planet.

A *Titan-Centaur*

[TI-tan-SEN-tor] rocket carried

Voyager 1 and 2 into space.

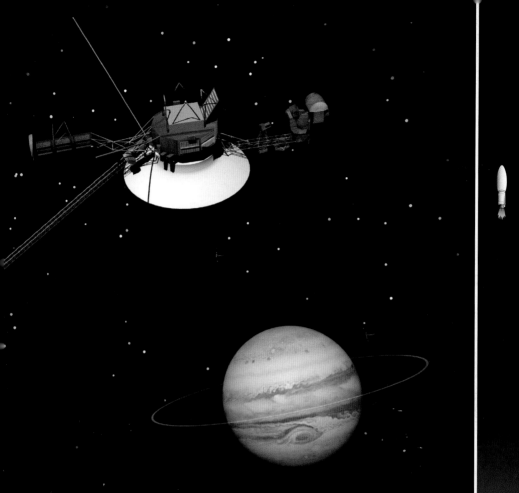

The *Voyager* probes have been flying for more than 35 years. Voyager 2 has flown past the planets Jupiter, Saturn, Uranus, and Neptune.

Voyager

The *Voyager* probes are
the farthest spacecraft
from Earth.

Neptune

Saturn

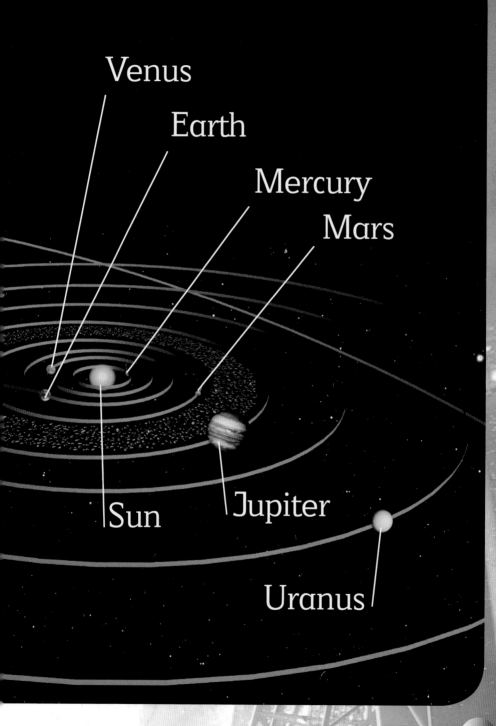

Venus

Earth

Mercury

Mars

Sun

Jupiter

Uranus

Chapter 4
Future Missions

Would you like to go
on a trip into space?

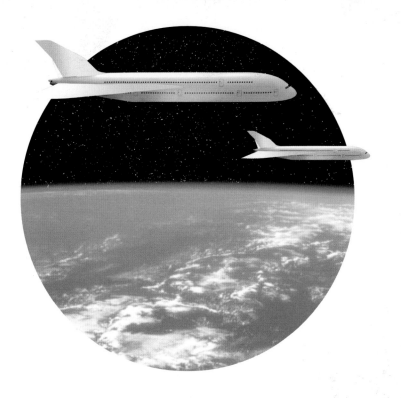

Spacecraft could soon take **passengers** on trips into sub-orbit. The passengers would feel like they are floating for a few minutes. Then the spacecraft would return to Earth.

There are many ideas for a future in space. Spaceplanes will take off from runways. Spacecraft will take passengers on trips to space hotels.

Spaceships will take astronauts to Mars and beyond.

Could this be the future for getting to Mars and living there? Would you like to be a space traveler?

Spaceship Gallery

These spaceships are not real. They appear in movies.

Rockets Quiz

1. In what year did the first person go into space?

2. Which is the largest rocket ever built?

3. How long have the *Voyager* probes been flying?

4. How many satellites can *Ariane 5* carry?

5. Where did the *Pathfinder* probe land?

Answers on page 45.

Glossary

astronaut person who has been trained to travel inside a spacecraft

booster part of a rocket that gives extra speed and power at lift off

capsule part of a spacecraft that people travel in, and often splits away from the rocket

lab (laboratory) place where science tests are carried out

orbit path an object makes around another object

passenger person who travels, but is not the driver

rover robotic vehicle that explores the surface of planets

spacecraft vehicle or probe designed to travel in space

space station space lab that orbits Earth with astronauts living there

Guide for Parents

DK Readers is a four-level interactive reading adventure series for children, developing the habit of reading widely for both pleasure and information. These books have an exciting main narrative interspersed with a range of reading genres to suit your child's reading ability. Each book is designed to develop your child's reading skills, fluency, grammar awareness, and comprehension in order to build confidence and engagement when reading.

Ready for a *Beginning to Read* book

YOUR CHILD SHOULD

- be familiar with using beginning letter sounds and context clues to figure out unfamiliar words.
- be aware of the need for a slight pause at commas and a longer one at periods.
- alter his/her expression for questions and exclamations.

A VALUABLE AND SHARED READING EXPERIENCE

For many children, reading requires much effort, but adult participation can make this both fun and easier. So here are a few tips on how to use this book with your child.

TIP 1 Check out the contents together before your child begins:

- read the text about the book on the back cover.
- flip through the book and stop to chat about the contents page together to heighten your child's interest and expectation.
- make use of unfamiliar or difficult words on the page in a brief discussion.
- chat about the nonfiction reading features used in the book, such as headings, captions, recipes, lists, or charts.

TIP 2 Support your child as he/she reads the story pages:

- give the book to your child to read and turn the pages.

- where necessary, encourage your child to break a word into syllables, sound out each one, and then flow the syllables together. Ask him/her to reread the sentence to check the meaning.

- when there's a question mark or an exclamation mark, encourage your child to vary his/her voice as he/she reads the sentence. Demonstrate how to do this if it is helpful.

TIP 3 Chat at the end of each page:

- the factual pages tend to be more difficult than the story pages, and are designed to be shared with your child.

- ask questions about the text and the meaning of the words used. These help to develop comprehension skills and awareness of the language used.

A FEW ADDITIONAL TIPS

- Always encourage your child to try reading difficult words by themselves. Praise any self-corrections, for example, "I like the way you sounded out that word and then changed the way you said it, to make sense."

- Try to read together everyday. Reading little and often is best. These books are divided into manageable chapters for one reading session. However, after 10 minutes, only keep going if your child wants to read on.

- Read other books of different types to your child just for enjoyment and information.

Series consultant, **Dr. Linda Gambrell**, Distinguished Professor of Education at Clemson University, has served as President of the National Reading Conference, the College Reading Association, and the International Reading Association.